MW00491276

Ninja Foodi XL Pro Air Oven Complete Cookbook

Quick, Delicious & Easy-to-Prepare Recipes to Air Fry, Bake, Roast, Pizza and More

(for Beginners and Advanced Users)

Lori Bullard

Table of Contents

Introduction

This comprehensive book is all about making some mouthwatering and delicious recipes using a versatile and unique appliance known as Ninja Foodi XL Pro Air Oven.

It is an addition to its previous ranged appliance, with remarkable features that make it stand up in market amongst competitors.

Now you do not need to buy multiple appliances to perform cooking, as it can bake, air fry, roast, bake, broil, toast, and bagel, dehydrate, and reheat. This appliance allows you to cook less fatty, healthy and crispy food without compromising health.

In this guide, we have included a meal plan along with 80 recipes so that all the Food lover can kick start the business, using the appliance and start making some mouthwatering meals with an odor free and hand free cooking experience.

After using the Ninja Foodi XL Pro Air Oven, you will be satisfied and get to know that why it is highest reviewed and rated on amazon.com.

This guide is for all family members and especially for a beginner.

It is a very effective cooking appliance that has some edge in terms of temperature, features, technology, which can be set with a touch of a button to do a variety of cooking.

Chapter 1: Breakfast Recipes

Cereal French toast

Prep Time: 15 Minutes | Cook Time: 20 Minutes | Makes: 6 Servings

Ingredients

- 14 ounces of coconut milk, sweetened
- 4 organic eggs
- ¼ teaspoon cinnamon
- 6 cups flake cereal, sugar-coated
- 6 slices brioche bread slices
- Cooking spray, for greasing
- ½ cup Maple syrup, for serving

Directions

1. Take a bowl and whisk eggs in it.
2. Then add coconut milk and cinnamon.
3. Now place cereal in a plastic bag and crush using a hand.
4. Add it to a shallow bowl.
5. Dip the bread in the milk then dredge in cereal.
6. Repeat the step for all bread slices.
7. Select the AIR Fry mode of Ninja Foodi XL Pro Air Oven and set the temperature to 425°F, for 15-20 minutes.
8. Press START to begin preheating.
9. Now oil sprays the Ninja Sheet Pan and places bread slices on it.
10. Air fry it in Ninja Foodi XL Pro Air Oven for 20 minutes
11. Remember to flip halfway through.
12. Once cooking is done, remove and serve with drizzle of maple syrup.

Serving Suggestion: Serve the toast with jam
Variation Tip: Use nutmeg instead of cinnamon for change of flavor
Nutritional Information per Serving: Calories 634 | Fat20.9 g |Sodium 582mg | Carbs 92.2 g| Fiber 4.2g | Sugar 55g | Protein 15.2g

French toast Sticks

Prep Time: 10 Minutes| Cook Time: 12 Minutes| Makes: 3 Servings

Ingredients

- 3 organic eggs
- 1/3 cup milk
- 1/3 teaspoon vanilla extract
- 1/3 teaspoon ground cinnamon
- 1/2 cup sugar, granulated
- 6 slices white bread, cut in thirds
- Oil spray, for greasing
- ½ cup Maple syrup, as needed

Directions

1. Take a bowl and whisk eggs in it.
2. Then pour in the milk along with cinnamon and vanilla extract.
3. Then add sugar and whisk all the ingredients well.
4. Take an air fryer basket and grease it with oil spray.
5. Dip the bread pieces into the egg mixture and then transfer it to the air fryer basket.
6.
7. Select start and preheat the Ninja Foodi XL Pro Air Oven at 400 degrees F for 12 minutes.
8. Once preheating done, Air fry the bread for 7 minutes, then press Start/pause to stop the Ninja Foodi XL Pro Air Oven.
9. Turn the bread and then again Air fry for 5 more minutes.
10. Once the cooking is complete, remove the basket and then drizzle maple syrup on top of toast.
11. Serve as a delicious breakfast.

Serving Suggestion: Serve the sticks with peanut butter
Variation Tip: Use brown sugar for change of flavor
Nutritional Information per Serving: Calories 390 | Fat 5.9g | Sodium 202mg | Carbs 79g | Fiber 0g | Sugar 67g | Protein 8g

Breakfast Hash

Prep Time: 10 Minutes | Cook Time: 20 Minutes | Makes: 6 Servings

Ingredients

- 1-1/2 -cups russet potatoes, peeled and cubed
- 2 kielbasa sausages, cubed
- 2 small yellow onions, peeled and chopped
- 1/3 cup carrots
- ¼ cup green beans
- 1/3 cup corn
- ¼ cup unsalted butter, melted
- 1 teaspoon paprika
- Salt and black pepper, to taste

Directions

1. Take a large bowl and add onion, potatoes, kielbasa, and all the vegetables, then pour in the melted butter to it.
2. Add salt, paprika, and black pepper.
3. Toss all the ingredients well.
4. Select BAKE function of Ninja Foodi XL Pro Air Oven by adjusting the temperature to 400 degrees F and set time to 20 minutes.
5. Press start so the preheating begins.
6. Transfer the ingredients to a ninja foodie sheet pan and bake it in Ninja Foodi XL Pro Air Oven until the cooking cycle completes.
7. Remember to shake the ingredient after 10 minutes.
8. Once done, serve and enjoy.

Serving Suggestion: Serve the hash with ketchup
Variation Tip: Sweet potatoes can be used as well
Nutritional Information per Serving: Calories 353 | Fat 29g | Sodium 726mg | Carbs10g | Fiber 1.8g | Sugar 2.1g | Protein 11g

Perfect Cinnamon Toast

Prep Time: 10 Minutes | Cook Time: 5 Minutes | Makes: 2 Servings

Ingredients

- 4 slices of whole wheat bread
- 4 tablespoons of salted butter, at room temperature
- 4 tablespoons of brown sugar, or to taste
- ½ teaspoon of cinnamon, ground
- ½ teaspoon of vanilla extract
- Pinch of salt

Directions

1. Select BAKE function of Ninja Foodi XL Pro Air Oven by adjusting the temperature to 400 degrees F and set time to 7 minutes.
2. Press start so the preheating begins.
3. In a bowl mix butter with sugar, cinnamon, and vanilla.
4. Add a pinch of salt as well.
5. Spread this mixture equally over the bread slices.
6. Put the coated bread slices on a sheet pan and place it inside Ninja Foodi XL Pro Air Oven.
7. Bake at 400 degrees F for 5 minutes.
8. Remove it from Ninja Foodi XL Pro Air Oven and serve.

Serving Suggestion: Serve the toast with peanut butter or almond butter
Variation Tip: Any bread variation can be used.
Nutritional Information per Serving: Calories 395 | Fat 24g | Sodium 506mg | Carbs 36.6g | Fiber 4g | Sugar 15.7g | Protein 7.5g

Breakfast Soufflé

Prep Time: 10 Minutes| Cook Time: 25 Minutes| Makes: 4 Servings

Ingredients

- 1/2 cup all-purpose flour
- 1/2 cup butter
- 1-1/4 cup almond milk
- ½ cup brown sugar
- 4 egg yolks
- 1 teaspoon vanilla extract
- ½ ounce of white sugar
- 1 teaspoon of cream of tartar
- Oil spray, for greasing

Directions

1. First press the start/pause button and turn on Ninja Foodi XL Pro Air Oven and set temperatures to 350 degrees F for 5 minutes.
2. Take a bowl and mix butter with flour.
3. In a saucepan pour milk and sugar and let it simmer over medium flame.
4. Then add flour mixture to the milk.
5. Cook it for 6 minutes and then let it get cool.
6. Next, grease the soufflé dishes with oil spray.
7. In a large mixing bowl whisk egg yolks, white sugar, vanilla extract and cream of tartar, and Pour this mixture into a soufflé dish and top it with a flour milk mixture.
8. Put the soufflé dish in the Ninja Foodi XL Pro Air Oven and then bake it for 18 minutes.
9. Once done, serve and enjoy.

Serving Suggestion: Serve with berries topping
Variation Tip: use dairy milk instead of almond milk
Nutritional Information per Serving: Calories 539 | Fat 42g | Sodium 187mg | Carbs 37g | Fiber 2g | Sugar 23g | Protein 5g

Breakfast Frittata Recipe

Prep Time: 10 Minutes| Cook Time: 13 Minutes| Makes: 4 Servings

Ingredients

- 4-5 large organic eggs
- 2 Italian sausages, chopped
- 2 cherry tomatoes, chopped
- Oil spray, for greasing
- 1/4 cup of parsley, chopped
- 1/2 cup of Parmesan cheese, per liking
- Salt and Black Pepper, to taste

Directions

1. The first step is to preheat the Ninja Foodi XL Pro Air Oven at 365 degrees F for 5 minutes
2. Use the baking pan of Ninja Foodi XL Pro Air Oven and add cherry tomatoes, and sausage to it.
3. Grease the ingredients with oil spray.
4. Place the pan in Ninja Foodi XL Pro Air Oven and cook it for 5 minutes.
5. Meanwhile, whisk the egg in a bowl and add parmesan cheese, parsley, salt, and pepper in it.
6. Take out the baking pan and transfer the ingredient to the egg mixture.
7. Bake in the oven for 8 minutes at 350 degrees F.
8. Once the eggs get firm, serve and enjoy.

Serving Suggestion: Serve with roasted potatoes
Variation Tip: Use cheese according to personal preference
Nutritional Information per Serving: Calories 371| Fat 29g | Sodium 748mg | Carbs 4g | Fiber 0g | Sugar 2g | Protein 21g

Avocado Eggs

Prep Time: 10 Minutes| Cook Time: 10 Minutes| Makes: 2 Servings

Ingredients

- 1 avocado, pitted
- 2 large eggs organic
- Salt and black pepper, to taste
- 2 bacon slices, cooked and chopped

Directions

1. Take an avocado and cut it in half.
2. Scoop some flesh out from the center.
3. Crack one egg in the center of the avocado and season it with salt and black pepper.
4. Place the egg into the baking tray.
5. Turn on the air roast function of Ninja Foodi XL Pro Air Oven by pressing the air roast mode.
6. Set time to 10 minutes at 375 degrees F.
7. Press the start, and when the timer beep put the tray inside the oven.
8. Once the cooking cycle complete, take out and serve with a sprinkle of bacon bits.

Serving Suggestion: Serve with slices of bread
Variation Tip: You can use turkey bacon to lower the calories
Nutritional Information per Serving: Calories 325 | Fat 27g| Sodium 478mg | Carbs 9 g | Fiber 6g | Sugar 0.7g | Protein 12.1g

Breakfast Oats

Prep Time: 10 Minutes| Cook Time: 17 Minutes| Makes: 2 Servings

Ingredients

- 1 cup steel-cut oats
- 2 cups of coconut milk
- 1 apple, peeled and chopped
- 2 tablespoons of brown sugar
- ½ teaspoon of cinnamon

Directions

1. Combine all the listed ingredients in a baking dish and mix well.
2. Place it inside Ninja Foodi XL Pro Air Oven and bake for 17 minutes at 360 degrees F.
3. Serve it as a hearty breakfast.

Serving Suggestion: Serve with mixed berries
Variation Tip: You can use dairy milk instead of coconut milk
Nutritional Information per Serving: Calories 726 | Fat 58g | Sodium 40mg | Carbs 51g | Fiber 10g | Sugar 28 g | Protein 8.8g

Delicious Egg and Cheese Muffins

Prep Time: 15 Minutes| Cook Time: 7 Minutes| Makes: 2 Servings

Ingredients

- 2 small organic eggs, whisked
- 2 tablespoons olive oil
- 75 ml of milk
- 100 grams of gluten-free flour
- 1 tablespoon baking powder
- ½ teaspoon of mustard powder
- 4 ounces of Parmesan, grated
- 1/4 teaspoon Worcestershire sauce
- Salt and black pepper, to taste

Equipment

- 8 paper muffin cases

Directions

1. Preheat the Ninja Foodi XL Pro Air Oven at 400 degrees F for 20 minutes.
2. Take 8 muffin cases and double up to make it 4 cups.
3. Take a bowl and whisk the eggs with olive oil and milk.
4. Then add the plain flour, mustard powder, baking powder, salt, black pepper, Worcestershire sauce, and Parmesan cheese.
5. Mix all the ingredients well.
6. Pour equal divided batter among 4 muffin cups.
7. Put the muffin cups on the baking tray.
8. Place it inside the Ninja Foodi XL Pro Air Oven, and close the lid.
9. Bake it for 5-7 minutes.
10. Once egg muffins are cooked, serve and enjoy.

Serving Suggestion: Serve it with cream cheese
Variation Tip: you can skip mustard powder if not like it.
Nutritional Information per Serving: Calories 565 | Fat 31g | Sodium 760mg | Carbs 48 g | Fiber 5g | Sugar 4g | Protein 27g

French toast Bread Pudding

Prep Time: 15 Minutes| Cook Time: 45 Minutes| Makes: 2 Servings

Ingredients

- 6 eggs, organic
- 3/4 cup heavy cream
- 2 tablespoons sugar
- 1 teaspoon orange liqueur
- Salt, to taste
- 2 cinnamon buns, broken in pieces
- 1/3 cup dried cherries

Directions

1. Take a bowl and whisk eggs in it.
2. Then add heavy cream, sugar, and mix well.
3. Then add orange liqueur, cherries, and salt.
4. Mix the ingredients for fine incorporation.
5. Now dredge the buns in the egg mixture.
6. Cover the bowl and refrigerate for 20 minutes.
7. Preheat the Ninja Foodi XL Pro Air Oven by select roasting for 3 minutes at 400 degrees.
8. Pour the refrigerated mixture into the ramekins.
9. Cover it with aluminum foil.
10. Put ramekins inside the oven.
11. Select ROAST, and adjust the temperature to 325 degrees F for 45 minutes.
12. Once the cooking cycle completely take out the pudding and serve.

Serving Suggestion: Serve it with cream cheese
Variation Tip: you can use any other flavored liquor of your choice
Nutritional Information per Serving: Calories 581 | Fat 31g | Sodium 321mg | Carbs 55g | Fiber 1.7g | Sugar 37g | Protein 18 g

Chapter 2: Snacks and Appetizers Recipes

Baked Apples

Prep Time: 15 Minutes| Cook Time: 45 Minutes| Makes: 2 Servings

Ingredients

- 2 gala apples, skin remove and cut in half
- 1 lemon, juice only
- 6 teaspoons light brown sugar
- 1/2 stick butter, cut into 16 pieces
- 10 teaspoons granulated sugar

TOPPINGS Ingredients

- 2 scoops Vanilla ice cream
- 2 tablespoons caramel syrup
- 2 tablespoons peanuts, chopped
- 6 vanilla wafers

Directions

1. Pierce the apples with the fork.
2. Take a basket and insert a crisper plate in it.
3. Preheat the Ninja Foodi XL Pro Air Oven by adjusting the temperature to 325 degrees F for 3 minutes.
4. Cover the basket with foil over the riper plate.
5. Put the apples on the foil and sprinkle lemon juice and brown sugar on top.
6. Put butter pieces on top as well.
7. Select air fry mode of Ninja Foodi XL Pro Air Oven and press start.
8. After 25 minutes remove the basket and sprinkle granulated sugar on apple pieces.
9. Again, press start and air fry for 20 minutes.
10. Once apples are baked, serve them with listed toppings.

Serving Suggestion: Serve it with ice-cream
Variation Tip: skip the sugar if want low Carb snack
Nutritional Information per Serving: Calories 743 | Fat 36.7g | Sodium 277mg | Carbs 100g | Fiber 3.5g | Sugar 89g | Protein 5.7g

Baked Loaded Potatoes

Prep Time: 15 Minutes| Cook Time: 40 Minutes| Makes: 2 Servings

Ingredients

- 2 large russet potatoes
- ¼ cup of cheddar cheese, shredded
- 8 ounces chili
- Salt, to taste

For Serving

- 2 tablespoons bacon bits
- 4 tablespoons sour cream

Directions

1. Pierce the potatoes and place them on a crisper plate, put the plate in the oven basket.
2. Select the bake and let it cook for 35 minutes at 390 degrees F.
3. Afterward, remove the potatoes and slice it.
4. Spoon the middle and add chilies and cheese.
5. Sprinkle salt on top.
6. Return the potatoes to the crisper plate.
7. Select the AIR FRY, set the temperature to 390 degrees F, and set the time to 4 minutes.
8. Once the cooking completes take out the potatoes and serve with the topping of bacon bits and sour cream.

Serving Suggestion: Serve it with cream cheese
Variation Tip: use turkey bacon instead of bacon bits.
Nutritional Information per Serving: Calories 833 | Fat 42g | Sodium 2259mg | Carbs74 g | Fiber 15g | Sugar 4g | Protein 40g

Beef Jerky

Prep Time: 15 Minutes| Cook Time: 7 hours| Makes: 2 Servings

Ingredients

- 1/3 cup soy sauce
- 1 tablespoon Worcestershire sauce
- 4 tablespoons dark brown sugar
- ½ teaspoon ground black pepper
- ½ teaspoon garlic powder
- ½ teaspoon onion powder
- 1 teaspoon paprika
- 1 teaspoon kosher salt
- 1 pound beef rib eye, uncooked and cut into 1/4-inch slices

Directions

1. Combine the entire listed ingredient in a bowl excluding beef.
2. Pour marinade into a plastic zip-lock bag.
3. Add beef to the zip-lock plastic bag and let the beef marinate in it for a few hours.
4. Afterward, take out the beef and drain excess liquid.
5. Remove the crisper plate from the basket of the oven and add meat.
6. Then put it back to the basket.
7. put basket in the oven.
8. Select the "DEHYDRATE" function and set the timer to 7 hours at 250 degrees F.
9. Once done, take out beef jerky and serve.

Serving Suggestion: fried rice
Variation Tip: you can use tamari sauce or coconut amino instead of soy sauce
Nutritional Information per Serving: Calories 572 | Fat 20g |Sodium 3788mg | Carbs 23 g | Fiber 1g | Sugar 20g | Protein 68g

Zucchini Crisps

Prep Time: 10 Minutes| Cook Time: 30 Minutes| Makes: 2 Servings

Ingredients

- 2 large zucchini, cut in sticks or round
- salt, to taste
- 1 cup all-purpose flour
- 3 eggs, beaten
- 2.5 cups bread crumbs
- 1/3 cup Parmesan cheese, grated
- 1 tablespoon garlic powder
- 1 teaspoon onion powder

Directions

1. Put zucchini in a bowl and add salt, let it sit for a while to drain excess liquid.
2. In a medium sized bowl mix the cheese, garlic powder, bread crumbs, onion powder, and salt.
3. Whisk the eggs in a bowl.
4. Place flour in a shallow bowl separately.
5. Toss zucchini in egg wash, then in flour, and at the end in bread crumb mixture.
6. Put it in a crisper plate and add it to the basket.
7. Put the basket in the Ninja Foodi XL Pro Air Oven.
8. Air fry at 360 degrees F for 30 minutes.
9. Halfway through toss the zucchini.
10. Once it's done, serve.

Serving Suggestion: Serve it with marinara sauce
Variation Tip: use Panko bread crumbs
Nutritional Information per Serving: Calories 864 | Fat 24g | Sodium 2277 mg | Carbs 116g | Fiber g | Sugar 7g | Protein 47 g

Brussels Sprouts With Bacon

Prep Time: 10 Minutes| Cook Time: 20 Minutes | Makes: 2 Servings

Ingredients

- 1 pound of Brussels sprouts
- 6 bacon strips
- 2 tablespoons of garlic powder
- 2 teaspoons of ginger powder
- salt and black pepper, to taste
- 1 tablespoon of olive oil

Directions

1. Press air fry and preheat the Ninja Foodi XL Pro Air Oven for 3 minutes at 390 degrees F.
2. Mix all the ingredients in a shallow bowl and then transfer it to the baking tray greased with oil spray.
3. Put the baking tray in the Ninja Foodi XL Pro Air Oven and air fry for 20 minutes.
4. Once half time passed, turn off the Ninja Foodi XL Pro Air Oven and take out the baking dish.
5. Shake the Brussels sprouts and then put it again in the Ninja Foodi XL Pro Air Oven.
6. Air fry until the time completes.
7. Serve.

Serving Suggestion: Serve it with mashed potatoes
Variation Tip: None
Nutritional Information per Serving: Calories 522 | Fat 37.9g | Sodium 809mg | Carbs 31g | Fiber 9.6g | Sugar 7g | Protein 24.3g

Mixed Nuts

Prep Time: 10 Minutes| Cook Time: 15 Minutes | Makes: 4 Servings

Ingredients

- 1 cup cashew
- 1/2 cup almond
- 1/2 cup peanut or walnuts
- ¼ cup honey
- Pinch of sea salt
- 1/3 teaspoon of paprika
- 1/2 teaspoon of cinnamon
- ½ cup brown sugar

Directions

1. In a bowl mix, all the ingredients listed above.
2. Transfer the nuts to the roasting pan.
3. Place pan inside a ninja oven.
4. Select bake and adjust the time to 15 minutes at 360degrees F.
5. Once nuts get roasted, take out and serve.

Serving Suggestion: Serve it with tea or coffee
Variation Tip: use personal preferred nuts.
Nutritional Information per Serving: Calories 503 | Fat 30g | Sodium 73mg | Carbs 52g | Fiber 4g | Sugar 38g | Protein 12g

Crispy Potatoes with Mayo

Prep Time: 10 Minutes| Cook Time: 25 Minutes | Makes: 2 Servings

Ingredients

- 1 pound baby potatoes, cut in slices
- 4 tablespoons olive oil
- 2 teaspoons hot paprika, divided
- 1 tablespoon smoked paprika, divided
- 1 tablespoon garlic powder, divided
- salt, to taste
- 1/2 cup mayonnaise

Directions

1. Take a mixing bowl and toss potatoes in it along with olive oil.
2. Add smoked paprika, hot paprika, garlic powder, and salt.
3. Select the air fry and preheat the ninja oven to 360 degrees F for 2 minutes.
4. Then place potatoes on a baking sheet or pan and put it in the oven.
5. Set temperature to 360 degrees F and set time to 25 minutes.
6. Halfway through remove the baking pan from the oven and toss the ingredients.
7. When cooking is complete, serve.

Serving Suggestion: Serve it with mayonnaise
Variation Tip: use any variation of potatoes you liked, it works fine with all the varieties.
Nutritional Information per Serving: Calories 625 | Fat 48g | Sodium 520 mg | Carbs 47g | Fiber 7g | Sugar 6.4g | Protein 7.6g

Jalapeno Poppers

Prep Time: 15 Minutes| Cook Time: 15 Minutes | Makes: 5 Servings

Ingredients

- 6 ounces of cream cheese, softened
- 6oucnes of shredded cheddar cheese
- salt, to taste
- 10jalapeño peppers, cut in half, seed removed
- 10 strips of bacon, uncooked

Direction

1. Preheat the oven by selecting AIR FRY at 360°F, for 3 minutes.
2. Meanwhile, take a mixing bowl and whisk together cheddar, salt, and cream cheese.
3. Fill the jalapeno paper with the cheese mixture.
4. Wrap each pepper with a bacon strip.
5. Place it on a grease baking pan.
6. Put the pan in the oven and set the timer to 15 minutes at 360 degrees F.
7. After 5 minutes, flip the poppers.
8. Once the cooking cycle complete, serve warm.

Serving Suggestion: Serve it with ranch
Variation Tip: you can use parmesan cheese instead of cheddar cheese.
Nutritional Information per Serving: Calories 551 | Fat50 g | Sodium 1523 mg | Carbs 4.1g | Fiber 1.1g | Sugar 1.2g | Protein 20g

French Fries

Prep Time: 10 Minutes| Cook Time: 20 Minutes | Makes: 2 Servings

Ingredients

- 1 pound of Idaho potatoes, cut into sticks
- salt, to taste
- 1 tablespoon of canola oil

Directions

1. Cut the potatoes into 2-inch strips and soak them in cold water for 30 minutes.
2. Drain and pat dry the potatoes.
3. Preheat the Ninja oven at 360 degrees F for 3 minutes.
4. Take a bowl and add potatoes, salt, and canola oil.
5. Toss all the ingredients well.
6. Transfer it to a baking dish and place it inside a ninja oven.
7. Set a timer to 25 minutes at 390 degrees F by selecting Bake.
8. After 15 minutes, turn off the oven and toss the fries.
9. Complete the cooking cycle.
10. Once 25 minutes pass, serve hot.

Serving Suggestion: Serve it with ketchup
Variation Tip: Use olive oil instead of canola oil
Nutritional Information per Serving: Calories 218 | Fat 5g |Sodium 91mg | Carbs 35g | Fiber 5g | Sugar 2g | Protein 2g

Blue Cheese Chicken Wings

Prep Time: 10 Minutes| Cook Time: 22 Minutes | Makes: 4 Servings

Ingredients

- 2 garlic cloves minced
- 1 teaspoon of mustard
- ½ teaspoon of Paprika powder
- Salt and black pepper to taste
- 4 tablespoons of canola oil
- Oil spray, for greasing
- 12 chicken wings
- 1 cup blue cheese, for coating

Directions

1. In a shallow bowl mix salt, garlic, black pepper, mustard, paprika, and canola oil.
2. Coat the chicken wings with the rub.
3. Take mesh basket and grease with oil spray.
4. Put the chicken wings into the mesh basket.
5. Preheat the Ninja oven at 357 degrees for 5 minutes.
6. After the preheating is done put the mesh basket in the Ninja Foodi XL Pro Air Oven.
7. Bake it for 22 minutes until crispy and brown from the top.
8. Once the chicken is cooked dredge it in blue cheese for fine coating.
9. Enjoy.

Serving Suggestion: Serve it with your favorite dipping sauce
Variation Tip: Use olive oil instead of canola oil
Nutritional Information per Serving: Calories 1080 | Fat 60g | Sodium 848mg | Carbs 1.1g | Fiber 0.1g | Sugar 0.2g | Protein 134g

Chapter 3: Fish and Seafood Recipes

Fish Sticks

Prep Time: 10 Minutes| Cook Time: 12 Minutes | Makes: 4 Servings

Ingredients

- 4 fish fillets, tilapia
- 1-1/2 cup all-purpose flour
- 3 large eggs, beaten
- 1 1/3 cups Panko bread crumbs
- Salt, to taste

Directions

1. Take a shallow bowl and put all-purpose flour in it.
2. Then take a separate bowl and whisk the egg in it.
3. Take a third bowl and mix bread crumbs with salt.
4. Coat the fish with flour then dredge with egg wash.
5. Then coat it with Panko bread crumbs.
6. Select air fry mode of Ninja Foodi XL Pro Air Oven and set the timer to 3 minutes at 400degrees F.
7. Now pace fish in a crisper basket and insert it in Ninja Foodi XL Pro Air Oven.
8. Select AIR FRY, and adjust the temperature to 390 degrees F for 12 minutes.
9. Remember to flip the fish halfway through.
10. Remove the fish and then serve.

Serving Suggestion: Serve it with tartar sauce
Variation Tip: you can use your favorite fish like salmon or Codfish.
Nutritional Information per Serving: Calories 521 | Fat 17.1 g | Sodium 840mg | Carbs 65.5 g| Fiber 2.9 g | Sugar 2.6 g | Protein 26.1g

Lemon & Herb Panko Crusted Cod

Prep Time: 10 Minutes| Cook Time: 15 Minutes | Makes: 4 Servings

Ingredients

- 2 uncooked cod fillets, (6 ounces each)
- 3 teaspoons kosher salt, divided
- 3/4 cup Panko bread crumbs
- 2 tablespoons butter, melted
- 1/4 cup fresh parsley, minced
- Zest and juice of 1 lemon

Directions

1. Put the crisper plate in the basket and put it in the oven and preheat to 360 degrees F for 3 minutes.
2. Now rub the fillets with salt.
3. Mix remaining ingredients in bowl and coat the fish with mixture.
4. Put the fish in the basket.
5. Bake it in Ninja Foodi XL Pro Air Oven for 15 minutes at 390 degrees F.
6. Select START/PAUSE and begin the cooking.
7. Once time complete, serve.
8. Enjoy.

Serving Suggestion: Serve it with ketchup or tartar sauce
Variation Tip: you can use olive oil instead of butter
Nutritional Information per Serving: Calories 192 | Fat 8g | Sodium 2155mg | Carbs 24g | Fiber 1.5g | Sugar 1g | Protein 8g

Coconut Fish Fillet

Prep Time: 10 Minutes| Cook Time: 8 Minutes | Makes: 4 Servings

Ingredients

- ½ cup sour cream
- 1 cup pineapple chunks, (liquid reserved)
- 2 eggs
- 1 cup cornstarch
- 2/3 cup sweetened coconut flakes
- 1-1/4 cup breadcrumbs
- 2 pounds large cod fish, thawed
- Olive oil, for misting

Directions

1. In a large bowl, combine the pineapple, and sour cream.
2. Mix it well and it aside for further use.
3. In a separate bowl whisk eggs and add pineapple liquid.
4. Put the cornstarch on a flat tray.
5. In a separate bowl mix breadcrumb and coconut flakes.
6. Dip the fish into cornstarch, then into the egg wash.
7. At the end dredge it into a crumb mixture.
8. Place the fish in Ninja Foodi XL Pro Air Oven by putting it into the baking tray.
9. Remember to spray it to oil spray.
10. Bake it for 8 minutes at 375 degrees F.
11. Serve with reserved sauce.

Serving Suggestion: Serve it with an additional dipping sauce of your type
Variation Tip: Use butter instead of olive oil.
Nutritional Information per Serving: Calories 524 | Fat 10g | Sodium 531mg | Carbs 59g | Fiber 2g | Sugar 6g | Protein 50g

Coconut Milk Shrimp

Prep Time: 10 Minutes| Cook Time: 15 Minutes | Makes: 4 Servings

Ingredients

- Salt and black pepper, to taste
- 1-1/2 pounds of shrimp
- 1 cup of coconut milk
- ¼ teaspoon of paprika, smoked
- 1/3 teaspoon of red chili flakes, to taste

Directions

1. Preheat the Ninja Foodi XL Pro Air Oven to 375 degrees F for 3 minutes.
2. Take a bow and mix coconut milk, salt, paprika, and red chili flakes.
3. Marinate the shrimp in the sauce for 2 hours.
4. Now put the shrimp in a baking tray and cover it with aluminum foil.
5. Turn on the Ninja Foodi XL Pro Air Oven and set the timer to 15 minutes at 375 degrees F at air fry mode.
6. Once fish is cooked, serve.

Serving Suggestion: Serve it with your favorite dipping sauce
Variation Tip: None
Nutritional Information per Serving: Calories 273 | Fat 16.2g | Sodium 286mg | Carbs 5.1g | Fiber1 g | Sugar 2g | Protein 27g

Fish Fillet

Prep Time: 10 Minutes| Cook Time: 12 Minutes | Makes: 4 Servings

Ingredients

- 1.5 cups breadcrumbs
- Salt, to taste
- Pepper, to taste
- 2 tablespoons fresh parsley
- 200 grams white fish fillet
- 1 cup plain all-purpose flour
- 3 eggs, whisked

Ingredients for Sauce

- 1 cup mayonnaise
- 1 tablespoon of capers, drained
- 2 jalapeños, chopped
- 2 tablespoons of lemon juice
- Pinch of chili flakes
- Salt, to taste

Directions

1. Mix sauce ingredients in a bowl and set aside for further use.
2. Preheat the Ninja Foodi XL Pro Air Oven to 375 degrees F for3 minutes.
3. In a bowl mix salt, pepper, parsley, bread crumb.
4. In a separate bowl, whisk eggs.
5. Put the flour in a flat tray.
6. Put the fillets first in the flour, then in the eggs, and at the end in the crumb.
7. Finely coat the fillets.
8. Cover a baking tray with aluminum foil.
9. Put the fish fillet on to the baking tray, skin side down.
10. Bake it in the oven for 12 minutes at 390 degrees F.
11. Serve and enjoy with sauce.

Serving Suggestion: Serve it with your favorite sauce if not preferred the listed one.
Variation Tip: None
Nutritional Information per Serving: Calories 784 | Fat 29g | Sodium 905mg | Carbs 49g | Fiber 2g | Sugar 6.2g | Protein 23g

Ginger Garlic Salmon

Prep Time: 10 Minutes| Cook Time: 13 Minutes | Makes: 4 Servings

Ingredients

- 2 pounds of salmon fillets
- Salt and black pepper, to taste
- 2 tablespoons of oyster sauce
- 2 tablespoons sugar
- 1 teaspoon cornstarch
- 2 cloves of garlic, minced
- 2-inch ginger, minced
- Red chili flakes, to taste
- 1 tablespoon of coconut amino

Directions

1. Take a baking tray and cover it with aluminum foil.
2. Put the fish fillet in the baking tray.
3. Take a bowl and mix coconut amino, oyster sauce, sugar, cornstarch, salt, red chili, pepper, ginger, and garlic paste.
4. Marinate the salmon in the sauce.
5. Then put it in a baking tray.
6. Turn on the Ninja Foodi XL Pro Air Oven and set the temperature at 350 degrees Fahrenheit. For 10 minutes.
7. Let the fish bake for 10 minutes.
8. Turn on broil for 3 minutes at 400 degrees Fahrenheit.
9. Then serve and enjoy.

Serving Suggestion: Serve it with your favorite dipping sauce
Variation Tip: Use olive oil as an addition to mist the fish
Nutritional Information per Serving: Calories 328 | Fat 14g | Sodium 155mg | Carbs 7.4g | Fiber 0.1g | Sugar 6g | Protein 44g

Tempura Batter Fish

Prep Time: 10 Minutes| Cook Time: 18 Minutes | Makes: 4 Servings

Ingredients

- 12 ounces cod fish fillet
- 1 cup Panko crumbs
- 1 lemon, wedges

Tempura Batter Ingredients

- 1 cup flour
- 11/3 cup corn starch
- 1 cup of water

Directions

1. Wash and pat dry the fish fillets.
2. In a bowl mix tempura batter.
3. Dredge the fish fillet into the tempura batter.
4. Then put it in Panko bread crumbs.
5. Place the fish fillet in a ninja oven baking tray and place it in the ninja oven.
6. Bake the fish fillet for 18 minutes at 390 degrees F.
7. Serve.

Serving Suggestion: Serve it with coleslaw
Variation Tip: None
Nutritional Information per Serving: Calories 744 | Fat 1.3g | Sodium 80mg | Carbs 161g | Fiber 1.1g | Sugar 0.1g | Protein 24g

Zesty Lemon Salmon

Prep Time: 15 Minutes| Cook Time: 12 Minutes | Makes: 3 Servings

Ingredients

- 1.5 pounds salmon fillet
- 1 teaspoon lemons, zest, and juice
- 4 tablespoons olive oil
- 1/2 teaspoon of turmeric
- 1/2 teaspoon of cumin
- ½ teaspoon of red chili flakes
- 1/2 teaspoon of oregano
- salt and black pepper

Directions

1. Take a baking tray and cover it with Aluminum foil.
2. Rub the salmon fillet with all the spices listed, and olive oil
3. Put Salmon on the baking tray.
4. Turn on the Ninja Foodi XL Pro Air Oven and set the temperature to 3 minutes, at 350 degrees Fahrenheit.
5. Afterward, put the baking tray in Ninja Foodi XL Pro Air Oven and bake it in the oven for 12 minutes.
6. Then serve and enjoy.

Serving Suggestion: Serve it with tartar sauce or sour cream
Variation Tip: Use canola oil or sesame oil instead of olive oil
Nutritional Information per Serving: Calories 464 | Fat 32g | Sodium 101mg | Carbs 0.7g | Fiber 0.3g | Sugar 0.1g | Protein 44g

Prawns Snack

Prep Time: 13 Minutes| Cook Time: 6 Minutes | Makes: 4 Servings

Ingredients

- 20 prawns
- 2 tablespoon of wine vinegar
- 2 teaspoon chili flakes
- Salt and black pepper, to taste
- 1 teaspoon of chili powder
- 6 teaspoons of ketchup

Directions

1. Preheat Ninja Foodi XL Pro Air Oven at 350 degrees F for 3 minutes.
2. In a bowl, mix all the spices and add prawns in it.
3. Coat the prawns well and then put it in a baking tray.
4. Select AIR FRY, and adjust the temperature to 390 degrees F for 6 minutes.
5. Once done, serve.

Serving Suggestion: Serve it with your favorite dipping sauce
Variation Tip: None
Nutritional Information per Serving: Calories 143 | Fat 2g | Sodium 459mg | Carbs 12 g | Fiber 0.8g | Sugar 2g | Protein 25g

Divine Salmon

Prep Time: 10 Minutes| Cook Time: 22 Minutes | Makes: 4 Servings

Ingredients

- 20 ounces of salmon fillets, 2 pieces
- 4 cloves of garlic, minced
- ½ tablespoon ginger, grated
- ½ tablespoon brown sugar
- 4 teaspoons sesame seeds
- 1/3 cup tamari sauce
- 1/3 cup water
- 1/3 cup dry sherry
- 4 tablespoons sesame oil

Directions

1. take a bowl and mix the tamari sauce, garlic, water, sesame oil, dry sherry, sesame seeds, ginger, and brown sugar in a bowl.
2. Mix ingredients in the bowl, until dissolve.
3. Place the salmon in a loaf pan and marinate the fish in this mixture for 30 minutes.
4. Now cover a baking tray with aluminum foil.
5. Put the fish fillet onto the baking tray.
6. Cover the dish with aluminum foil.
7. Put the tray inside the oven.
8. Turn on the ninja oven at 390 degrees for 18 minutes, by selecting air fry.
9. Let it cook; remember to flip the fish halfway through.
10. afterward, turn on the broil and take off the aluminum for the top of the fish
11. bake it for 4 more minutes
12. then take out and serve

Serving Suggestion: Serve it with tartar sauce
Variation Tip: Use olive oil instead of sesame oil
Nutritional Information per Serving: Calories 1179 | Fat 35g | Sodium 1164mg | Carbs 51g | Fiber 1g | Sugar 2g | Protein 156.6g

Bake Clams

Prep Time: 10 Minutes| Cook Time: 3 Minutes | Makes: 6 Servings

Ingredients

- 1 cup bread crumb
- ½ cup parmesan
- 1.2 cups parsley
- ½ teaspoon of lemon zest
- 6 tablespoons of butter, melted
- 2 garlic cloves
- 2 dozen clams
- salt and black pepper, to taste

Directions

1. Take a heat proof Shallow bowl and combine Parmesan cheese, breadcrumbs, lemon zest garlic, parsley, and melted butter.
2. Mix the ingredients well and then place this mixture on top of the exposed clams.
3. Season it with salt and black pepper.
4. put in a Ninja Foodi XL oven.
5. Then press start button of Ninja Foodi XL Pro Air Oven.
6. Adjust the cooking time to 2-3 minutes at 400 degrees F.
7. Bake the clams until time completes.
8. One done, serve.

Serving Suggestion: Serve it with lemon wedges
Variation Tip: Use olive oil instead of melted butter.
Nutritional Information per Serving: Calories 286 | Fat 16.4g | Sodium 395mg | Carbs 16g | Fiber 1.3g | Sugar 2g | Protein 18g

Prawns Snack

Prep Time: 10 Minutes| Cook Time: 8 Minutes | Makes: 2 Servings

Ingredients

- 10 fresh king prawns
- 1 tablespoon of wine vinegar
- 4 tablespoons of mayonnaise
- 1 teaspoon of ketchup
- 1 teaspoon chili flakes
- 1/3 teaspoon of sea salt
- 1/3 teaspoon of ground black pepper
- 1 teaspoon of chili powder
- 1 teaspoon of canola oil

Directions

1. Preheat the Ninja Foodi XL Pro Air Oven at 360 degrees F for 3 minutes.
2. Mix all the ingredients in a shallow bowl and coat the prawns well.
3. Transfer it to a baking tray and bake it in Ninja Foodi XL Pro Air Oven for 8 minutes.
4. Once done, serve.

Serving Suggestion: Serve it with your favorite dipping sauce
Variation Tip: Use olive oil instead of canola oil
Nutritional Information per Serving: Calories 276 | Fat 14g | Sodium 93mg | Carbs 19.0 g | Fiber 1g | Sugar 3.5g | Protein 25g

Chapter 4: Poultry Mains Recipes

Spice-Rubbed Chicken Breasts with Chimichurri

Prep Time: 15 minutes | Cook Time: 35 minutes | makes: 2 servings

Ingredients

- salt and black pepper, to taste
- ½ tablespoon paprika
- 1 tablespoon chili powder
- 2 tablespoons ground fennel
- 2 teaspoons onion powder
- 1 teaspoon garlic powder
- ½ teaspoon ground cumin
- 2 chicken breasts, uncooked
- 2 tablespoons canola oil

CHIMICHURRI Ingredients

- 1/3 cup olive oil
- 1/3 bunch fresh cilantro
- 1/3 bunch fresh parsley
- 2 shallots, peeled, cut in quarters
- 5 cloves garlic, peeled
- Zest and juice of 1 lemon
- salt, to taste

Directions

1. In a large bowl mix all the dry spices including salt, paprika, chili powder, fennel, black pepper, onion powder, garlic powder, and cumin.
2. Rub the chicken breasts with the dry rub.
3. Coat the chicken with canola oil.
4. Put the crisper plate in the oven basket and put it in Ninja Foodi XL Pro Air Oven.
5. Preheat oven by selecting AIR FRY, at 300 degrees F for 3 minutes.
6. Afterward, select air fry mode and adjust time to35 minutes at 300 degrees F.
7. Put the chicken in the basket and cook until the cooking cycle complete.
8. Meanwhile, combine all the Chimichurri ingredients in a ninja blender and pulse into a paste.
9. Afterward, remove chicken from the basket and serve with Chimichurri sauce.

Serving Suggestion: Serve it with ranch dressing
Variation Tip: Use olive oil instead of canola oil
Nutritional Information per Serving: Calories 750 | Fat 60.2g | Sodium 251mg | Carbs 12g | Fiber 4g | Sugar 1.7g | Protein 45g

Yogurt Chicken

Prep Time: 15 minutes | Cook Time: 35minutes | makes: 2 servings

Ingredients

- 3-4 chicken breasts
- 1/3 cup yogurt
- 1/2 teaspoon cumin
- 1/4 teaspoon turmeric
- 1/4 teaspoon red chili flakes
- 1/3 teaspoon lemon zest
- 1/4 teaspoon black pepper
- salt, to taste
- oil spray, for greasing

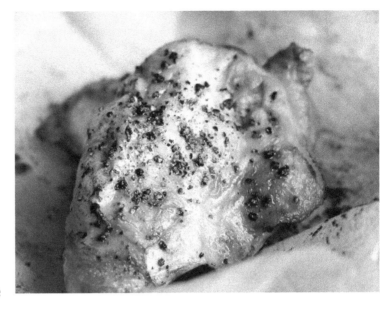

Directions

1. Combine yogurt with listed spices and ingredients.
2. Marinate chicken breast in the marinate.
3. Let it sit for 20 minutes.
4. Preheat the Ninja Foodi XL Pro Air Oven by selecting AIR FRY, at 300 degrees F for 3 minutes.
5. After preheating is complete, select air fry mode and adjust the time to 35 minutes at 310 degrees F.
6. Put the chicken breast in oil greased baking sheet pan and place it in ninja oven.
7. Once done, serve.

Serving Suggestion: Serve it with chili sauce
Variation Tip: Use vinegar instead of lemon zest
Nutritional Information per Serving: Calories 451 | Fat 17.6g | Sodium 296mg | Carbs 3.5g | Fiber 0.2g | Sugar 2.9g | Protein 65g

Chicken Tikka Masala

Prep Time: 15 minutes | Cook Time: 25 minutes | makes: 2 servings

Ingredients

- 1 pound chicken breasts, chopped into bite-size pieces
- 1/3 cup fat-free Greek yogurt
- 1 teaspoon Garam Masala
- 2 tablespoons lemon juice
- Salt and black pepper, to taste
- 1/4 teaspoon ginger, powder
- 2 tablespoons of olive oil

Directions

1. In a bowl mix, all the ingredients coat the chicken breasts with the rub.
2. Put the crisper plate in the frying basket and put it in Ninja Foodi XL Pro Air Oven.
3. Preheat oven by selecting AIR FRY, at 300 degrees F for 5 minutes.
4. Select air fry mode and adjust time to25 minutes at 350 degrees F.
5. Put the chicken in a basket and air fry in Ninja Foodi XL Pro Air Oven once done, take out the chicken and serve.

Serving Suggestion: Serve it with your favorite dipping sauce
Variation Tip: Use canola oil instead of olive oil
Nutritional Information per Serving: Calories 655 | Fat 30g | Sodium 265mg | Carbs 7.5g | Fiber 7g | Sugar 7.3g | Protein 84g

Honey Sriracha Lime Chicken Wings

Prep Time: 15 minutes | Cook Time: 25 minutes | makes: 4 servings

Ingredients

- 4 tablespoons Sriracha sauce
- 1/3 cup honey
- 4 tablespoons soy sauce
- 2 tablespoons brown sugar
- ½ tablespoon ground ginger
- Zest and juice of 2 limes
- 2.5 pounds chicken wings

Directions

1. Take a bowl and combine wings with listed ingredients.
2. refrigerate it for at least 1-hour
3. Turn on the air fry mode of Ninja Foodi XL Pro Air Oven and set the temperature to 400 degrees F for 25 minutes.
4. once preheating done, add chicken to a sheet pan and cook for 25 minutes
5. After 10 minutes of cooking use a tong to flip the chicken wings.
6. cook for additional 15 minutes
7. Once done, take out the chicken and serve.

Serving Suggestion: Serve it with blue cheese or ranch
Variation Tip: Use lemons instead of lime
Nutritional Information per Serving: Calories 652 | Fat 22g | Sodium 1148mg | Carbs 30g | Fiber 0.3g | Sugar 28g | Protein 83g

Buffalo wings

Prep Time: 15 Minutes | Cook Time: 25 Minutes | Makes: 2 Servings

Ingredients

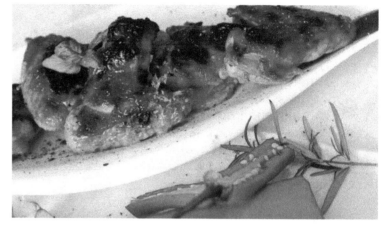

- 8 chicken wings
- 2 tablespoons butter
- 1/4 cup hot sauce
- 1 clove of garlic, minced
- 1/4 teaspoon paprika
- 1/4 teaspoon cayenne pepper
- Salt and black pepper, to taste

Directions

1. Take a bowl and combine all the listed ingredients.
2. Marinate the chicken wings in it for 20 minutes.
3. Turn on the air fry mode of Ninja Foodi XL Pro Air Oven and set the temperature to 375 degrees F for 2 minutes.
4. Once preheating done, add chicken wings to the oil greased sheet pan.
5. Turn on air frying mode and set the timer to 20 minutes.
6. After10 minutes of cooking use a tong to flip the chicken wings.
7. Once the cooking cycle completes, serve, and enjoy.

Serving Suggestion: Serve it with your favorite dipping sauce
Variation Tip: Use olive oil instead of butter.
Nutritional Information per Serving: Calories 606 | Fat 27g | Sodium 292mg | Carbs 0g | Fiber 0.3g | Sugar 0.4g | Protein 84g

Country Style Chicken Wings

Prep Time: 20 Minutes | Cook Time: 25 Minutes | Makes: 4 Servings

Ingredients

- 2 pounds of chicken wings
- 10 ounces of Plum sauce
- 1/3 cup brown sugar
- 6 tablespoons soy sauce
- 2 tablespoons cornstarch
- 1/3 cup orange juice
- Salt and pepper, to taste

Directions

1. Take a bowl and combine all the listed ingredients.
2. Marinate it for 20 minutes.
3. Turn on the air fry mode and set the temperature to 375 degrees F for 2 minutes.
4. Once preheating done, add chicken wings to a sheet pan.
5. Turn on the air frying mode of Ninja Foodi XL Pro Air Oven and set the timer to 20 minutes.
6. After10 minutes of cooking use a tong to flip the chicken wings.
7. Once the cooking cycle completes, serve, and enjoy.

Serving Suggestion: Serve it with your favorite dipping sauce
Variation Tip: Use lemon juice instead of orange juice.
Nutritional Information per Serving: Calories 522 | Fat 18g | Sodium 1552mg | Carbs 21g | Fiber 0.5g | Sugar 15g | Protein 68g

Roasted Chicken with Apple

Prep Time: 20 minutes | Cook Time: 25 minutes | makes: 4 servings

Ingredients

- 3 gala apples, peeled and sliced
- 6 tablespoons unsalted butter
- 2 tablespoons orange zest
- 1 teaspoon cinnamon
- 1.5 pounds of whole chicken, pieces or cut in half
- Salt and black pepper, pinch
- 2 teaspoons of ginger garlic paste
- Olive oil, for greasing

Directions

1. Grease a ninja oven baking pan with olive oil.
2. Cover the bottom of the pan with slices of apple.
3. Take a bowl and combine, cinnamon, butter, zest, ginger garlic paste, salt, and black pepper.
4. Rub the chicken pieces with the mixture.
5. Put the chicken on the top of apple slices in the oven pan.
6. Turn on the Ninja Foodi XL Pro Air Oven and set the timer to 25 minutes at 390 degrees F.
7. Roast the chicken until internal temperature reaches 165 degrees F.
8. Serve the chicken with caramelized apples from the bottom.
9. Enjoys hot.

Serving Suggestion: Serve it with coleslaw
Variation Tip: None
Nutritional Information per Serving: Calories 529 | Fat 37g | Sodium 260mg | Carbs 13.3 g| Fiber 2.1g | Sugar 10g | Protein 30g

Tarragon-Mustard Chicken

Prep Time: 20 minutes | Cook Time: 25 minutes | makes: 2 servings

Ingredients

- 1 pound chicken breast, cubed
- 2 tablespoons of olive oil, melted
- 2 tablespoons Dijon mustard
- 2 teaspoons dried tarragon leaves
- 2 teaspoons sugar
- 1 teaspoon lemon juice
- Salt and pepper, to taste
- oil spray, for greasing

Direction

1. Take a Ninja Foodi XL Pro Air Oven baking pan and grease it with oil spray.
2. Take a bowl and combine olive oil, Dijon mustard, tarragon leaves, sugar, lemon juice, salt, pepper.
3. Coat the chicken breast with the rub.
4. Turn on the ninja oven and set the timer to 5 minutes at 390 degrees F.
5. Once preheating done, put the chicken in the baking pan /sheet and put it in Ninja Foodi XL Pro Air Oven and air fry for 25 minutes at 390 degrees F.
6. Once done, serve.

Serving Suggestion: Serve it with ketchup
Variation Tip: Use stevia instead of sugar
Nutritional Information per Serving: Calories 500 | Fat 20g | Sodium 250mg | Carbs 5.2g | Fiber0.6g | Sugar 4.2g | Protein 48g

Cheesy Chicken

Prep Time: 15 minutes | Cook Time: 12 minutes | makes: 2 servings

Ingredients

- 1 pound chicken breasts cut into cubes
- 2 tablespoons olive oil
- Avocado, sliced
- Sour cream, for garnish
- 1 cup cheddar cheese, shaving

Ingredients for Nacho Seasoning

- ½ tablespoon fresh lemon juice
- ½ tablespoon fresh lime juice
- ½ teaspoon ground cumin
- 1/2 cup fresh cilantro, finely chopped
- 2 teaspoons onion powder
- 2 teaspoons chili powder
- Salt, to taste

Directions

1. Take a bowl and mix oil and chicken in it.
2. Then add all the nacho seasoning to the bowl.
3. Select the air roast of the Ninja Foodi XL Pro Air Oven and set the temperature to 350 degrees F, for 15 minutes.
4. Once preheating complete add chicken to a pan and put it in the oven.
5. Air roast for 12 minutes at 350 degrees F.
6. Once done, remove it from the oven and serve with sour cream, cheese, and avocado.

Serving Suggestion: Serve it with tortilla chips
Variation Tip: Use personally preferred cheese.
Nutritional Information per Serving: Calories 984 | Fat 69g | Sodium 525mg | Carbs 9 g | Fiber 0.7g | Sugar 0.8g | Protein 81 g

Cajun Spice Chicken

Prep Time: 15 Minutes | Cook Time: 20 Minutes | Makes: 2 Servings

Ingredients

- 1 pound chicken breast, uncooked and skinless
- 2 tablespoons oil, divided
- 2 tablespoons Cajun seasoning
- 3 sweet potatoes, peeled, cut into cubes
- 1 cup broccoli cut in florets
- Salt and black pepper

Directions

1. Take a bowl and add oil and Cajun seasoning.
2. Rub the chicken breast with the rub.
3. Put the chicken in the ninja foodie pan along with broccoli and sweet potatoes.
4. Sprinkle salt and black pepper on top.
5. Turn on the Ninja Foodi XL Pro Air Oven and select air roast.
6. Set a timer to 20 minutes at 400 degrees F.
7. Once preheating done, add the chicken pan to the oven.
8. When the internal temperature of the chicken reaches 165 degrees F, serve it, and enjoy it.

Serving Suggestion: Serve it with your favorite dipping sauce or rice
Variation Tip: None
Nutritional Information per Serving: Calories 562 | Fat 18.4 g | Sodium 388mg | Carbs 42.3g | Fiber 7g | Sugar 9g | Protein 52g

Chicken Stir Fry

Prep Time: 15 Minutes | Cook Time: 25 Minutes | Makes: 2 Servings

Ingredients

- 1 pound chicken breasts cut into cubes
- 2 red bell pepper, thinly sliced
- ½ yellow bell pepper, thinly sliced
- 2 orange bell pepper, thinly sliced
- 1 carrot, thinly sliced
- 1/4 cup stir fry sauce
- ¼ cup corn, drained
- ½ cup broccoli, cut in florets
- 2 teaspoons sesame seeds, for garnish
- oil spray, for greasing

Direction

1. Take a bowl and add chicken, bell peppers, corn, broccoli, and carrots in a bowl.
2. Use an oil spray to coat the ingredient with oil.
3. Put the ingredients in a ninja sheet pan.
4. Turn on the air roast and set the timer to 25 minutes at 400 degrees F.
5. Garnish with sesame seeds and stir fry sauce.

Serving Suggestion: Serve it with your favorite dipping sauce
Variation Tip: Use olive oil instead of oil spray.
Nutritional Information per Serving: Calories 525 | Fat 19g | Sodium 230mg | Carbs 17g | Fiber 3.8g | Sugar 8.5g | Protein 67g

Chicken Meat Patties

Prep Time: 15 Minutes | Cook Time: 20 Minutes | Makes: 3 Servings

Ingredients

- 1.5 pounds of chicken meat, ground
- 1 tablespoon of olive oil
- ½ cup shallots, chopped
- 2 green peppers, chopped
- 1 teaspoon coriander powder
- ½ teaspoon of turmeric
- ¼ teaspoon of cumin, ground
- 1 egg, whisked
- salt, to taste

Directions

1. Take a shallow bowl and mix all the ingredients.
2. Make meat patties of the mixture and place it on a baking sheet that is greased with oil spray.
3. Bake it in Ninja Foodi XL Pro Air Oven for20 minutes at 400 degrees F.
4. Once done, serve.

Serving Suggestion: Serve it with your favorite dipping sauce
Variation Tip: Use olive oil instead of canola oil
Nutritional Information per Serving: Calories 529 | Fat 23g | Sodium 272 mg | Carbs 5.6g | Fiber 1.5g | Sugar 2g | Protein 68g

Teriyaki Glazed Chicken

Prep Time: 15 Minutes | Cook Time: 22 Minutes | Makes: 4 Servings

Ingredients

- 2 pounds chicken, boneless
- oil spray, for greasing

Teriyaki Glaze Ingredients

- ¼ cup Soy Sauce
- ¼ cup Japanese cooking wine
- ½ cup Brown Sugar
- 2tablespoons of Lime Juice
- 1/2 cup Orange Juice
- 1 teaspoon of ginger, ground
- ½ teaspoon garlic

Directions

1. Mix all the teriyaki glaze ingredients in a shallow bowl and add chicken pieces to it.
2. Let it marinate for a few minutes.
3. Now preheat the ninja oven at 392 degrees F for 5 minutes.
4. Use a baking sheet/ pan and grease it with oil spray.
5. add chicken pieces along with sauce to the pan and put the pan in Ninja Foodi XL Pro Air Oven air fry at 400 for 20 -22 minutes.
6. Once done, serve and enjoy.

Serving Suggestion: Serve it with mashed potatoes
Variation Tip: Use can skip the sugar if do not like the sweet touch.
Nutritional Information per Serving: Calories 437 | Fat 7g | Sodium 1047mg | Carbs 22g | Fiber 0.3g | Sugar 20g | Protein 67g

Whole Chicken Roast

Prep Time: 15 Minutes | Cook Time: 25-30 minutes | Makes: 4 Servings

Ingredients

- 2.5 pounds chicken, whole
- ½ cup canola oil
- 1 teaspoon red pepper flakes
- 2 teaspoons of Brown Sugar
- 2 lemons juice
- 1 teaspoon of cumin
- 1 teaspoon of paprika
- 1teasppoon of lemon zest
- 2 teaspoons thyme, chopped
- 1 teaspoon d rosemary, chopped
- Salt and fresh black pepper, to taste

Directions

1. Cut the chicken from the top by placing it on a cutting board.
2. Remove the backbone of the chicken.
3. now in a shallow bowl mix all the listed ingredients along with chicken
4. Rub the chicken with ingredients.
5. Preheat the Ninja Foodi XL Pro Air Oven to 400 degrees F for 5 minutes.
6. Then transfer the chicken to the baking pan cover with aluminum foil.
7. Air roast the chicken in the oven for 25 minutes at 390 degrees F.
8. After25 minutes check and cook for a few minutes more if needed then serve by resting for a while.

Serving Suggestion: Serve it with your favorite dipping sauce
Variation Tip: None
Nutritional Information per Serving: Calories 681 | Fat 36g | Sodium 181mg | Carbs 2.6g | Fiber 0.6g | Sugar 1.6g | Protein 82g

BBQ Chicken Wings

Prep Time: 15 minutes | Cook Time: 25 minutes | makes: 4 servings

Ingredients

- 6 tablespoons BBQ sauce
- 2 tablespoon brown sugar
- ½ tablespoon ginger powder
- salt and black pepper, to taste
- ½ teaspoon of paprika
- 1/3 cup honey
- 2.5 pounds chicken wings

Directions

1. In a large bowl mix BBQ sauce. Brown sugar, honey, paprika, salt, black pepper, and ginger powder.
2. Marinate chicken wings in it for few hours.
3. Preheat the ninja oven for 3 minutes at 400 degrees.
4. Transfer the wings from the bowl to the baking tray.
5. Air roast the wing in ninja oven for 25 minutes.
6. After10 minutes of cooking use tongs to flip the chicken wings.
7. Once cooking is complete and wings are done, take out the chicken and serve.

Serving Suggestion: Serve it with your favorite dipping sauce
Variation Tip: Use olive oil to mist the wings.
Nutritional Information per Serving: Calories 680 | Fat 21.2g | Sodium 500mg | Carbs 36.6g | Fiber 0.4g | Sugar 33.7g | Protein 82g

Turkey in Ninja Oven

Prep Time: 15 minutes | Cook Time: 25 minutes | makes: 2 servings

Ingredients

- 1 pound turkey breast, rib removed
- 2 tablespoon olive oil
- salt, to taste
- 2 tablespoons dry turkey seasoning

Directions

1. Rub the turkey breast with olive oil, salt, and dry turkey seasoning.
2. Preheat the Ninja Foodi XL Pro Air Oven at 350 degrees F for 3 minutes.
3. Put the crisper plate in the oven basket and put it in the unit.
4. Preheat oven by selecting AIR FRY, at 300 degrees F for 3 minutes.
5. Then select air fry mode and adjust the time to 35 minutes at 310 degrees F.
6. Put the turkey breasts in the basket and cook until the cycle complete.
7. Let it rest for10 minutes, before serving.

Serving Suggestion: Serve it with your favorite dipping sauce or mashed potatoes
Variation Tip: None
Nutritional Information per Serving: Calories 356 | Fat 17.8g | Sodium 2380mg | Carbs 9.6g | Fiber 1.1g | Sugar 8g | Protein 38.7g

Chapter 5: Dessert Recipes

Air Broil Bananas

Prep Time: 15 minutes | Cook Time: 6 minutes | makes: 2 servings

Ingredients

- 2 tablespoons dark brown sugar
- ½ teaspoon ground cinnamon
- 3 firm bananas, half lengthwise

Directions

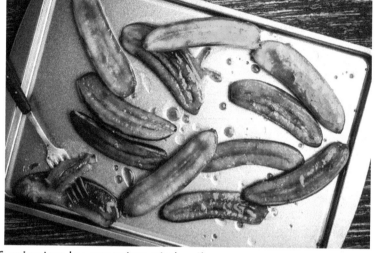

1. Take a bowl and mix brown sugar with cinnamon.
2. Coat the bananas with cinnamon and sugar.
3. Put the banana on a ninja sheet pan and set the timer to 6 minutes by pressing air broil.
4. Once bananas are done, serve.

Serving Suggestion: Serve it with ice-cream or whipping cream
Variation Tip: skip the sugar if want low Carb snack
Nutritional Information per Serving: Calories 193 | Fat 0.6 | Sodium 4mg | Carbs 50g | Fiber 5g | Sugar 30g | Protein 2g

Red Velvet Cookies

Prep Time: 15 minutes | Cook Time: 22 minutes | makes: 4 servings

Ingredients

- 1 -1/2 cups all-purpose flour
- 4 tablespoons unsweetened cocoa powder
- 1 teaspoon baking soda
- pinch of salt
- 1/3 cup butter, softened
- 3/4 cup brown sugar
- 1/3 cup granulated sugar
- 2 eggs, whisked
- 1 tablespoon cream cheese
- 1 tablespoon milk
- 1 teaspoon vanilla extract
- 1 tablespoon red food coloring
- 6 ounces white chocolate chips

Directions

1. Take a bowl and mix cocoa powder, salt, flour, baking soda and set it as die for further use.
2. In a separate bowl beat cream butter, brown sugar then adds in the eggs and keeps on mixing with hand beater.
3. Then add cream cheese, vanilla, food coloring, and milk.
4. Add dry ingredients to the blended egg mixture.
5. Then fold in white chocolate chips.
6. Put 9 cookies on the Ninja® Sheet Pan.
7. Bake for 22miutes at 350 degrees F in the oven.
8. Once done, take out and serve.

Serving Suggestion: Serve it with coffee
Variation Tip: skip the sugar if want low Carb snack
Nutritional Information per Serving: Calories 706 | Fat 39 | Sodium 500mg | Carbs 95g | Fiber 2.7g | Sugar 68g | Protein 10.1g

Walnut Chocolate Cookies

Prep Time: 15 minutes | Cook Time: 20 minutes | makes: 4 servings

Ingredients

- 1 -1/2 cups all-purpose flour
- 4 tablespoons unsweetened cocoa powder
- 1 teaspoon baking soda
- 1/3 cup butter, softened
- 3/4 cup brown sugar
- 2 eggs
- 4 tablespoons milk
- 1 teaspoon vanilla extract
- 6 ounces walnuts, chopped

Directions

1. Take a bowl and mix cocoa powder, flour, baking soda and mix.
2. In a separate bowl beat eggs, with butter and sugar.
3. Then add vanilla and milk.
4. Add dry ingredients to the blended egg mixture.
5. Then fold in walnuts.
6. Put cookie shapes on the Ninja® Sheet Pan.
7. Put the ninja sheet pan in the oven.
8. Bake for 20 minutes at 350 degrees F.
9. Once done, take out and serve.

Serving Suggestion: Serve it with coffee
Variation Tip: skip the sugar if want low Carb snack
Nutritional Information per Serving: Calories 670 | Fat 44 | Sodium 472mg | Carbs 58.7g | Fiber 5.5gv| Sugar 28g | Protein 18g

Banana Cupcake

Prep Time: 15 minutes | Cook Time: 22 minutes | makes: 4 servings

Ingredients

- 1.5 cups old fashioned oats
- Pinch ground nutmeg
- ½ teaspoon baking powder
- Pinch of salt
- 1 large egg
- 1/2 cup mashed bananas
- ¼ teaspoon pure vanilla extract
- ½ cup almond milk
- 4 tablespoons of sugar

Directions

1. Preheat the ninja's oven to 350 degrees for 5 minutes.
2. In a mixing bowl, combine nutmeg, baking powder, sugar, salt, and oats.
3. In a separate bowl, whisk the egg and mix the vanilla extract, and bananas.
4. Then pour in almond milk and butter into the egg mixture.
5. Keep on mixing until finely combined.
6. Now combine ingredients of both the bowl.
7. Place the scoop full into grease muffin pan.
8. Bake muffins, for 22 minutes at 350 degrees F.
9. Once it's done, serve.

Serving Suggestion: Serve it with ice-cream
Variation Tip: skip the sugar if want low Carb snack
Nutritional Information per Serving: Calories 512 | Fat 26 | Sodium 71mg | Carbs 62g | Fiber 9g | Sugar 19g | Protein 11.2g

Chocolate Peanut Butter Cupcakes

Prep Time: 15 minutes | Cook Time: 25 minutes | makes: 4 servings

Ingredients

- 2 cups chocolate cake mix
- 1 large egg
- 3 egg yolks
- 1/4 cup olive oil
- 1/3 cup water, hot
- 1/4 cup sour cream
- 6 tablespoons of peanut butter
- 4 tablespoons of sugar

Directions

1. Take 20 muffin cups and double them up into make 10
2. Grease a baking pan with oil spray.
3. Set it aside for further use.
4. Take a large bowl and whisk egg, egg yolk, cake mix, olive oil, hot water, and sour cream.
5. Use a hand beater to beat it.
6. In a separate large bowl, mix peanut butter and white sugar.
7. Equally pour chocolate batter into muffin cups and top it with peanut butter mixture.
8. Bake for 15 minutes at 300 degrees F in ninja oven.
9. Serving Suggestion: Serve it with ice-cream.

Variation Tip: Skip the sugar if want low Carb snack
Nutritional Information per Serving: Calories 740 | Fat 44 | Sodium 843mg | Carbs 80g | Fiber 3.5g | Sugar 47g | Protein 15.1g

Apple Crisp

Prep Time: 15 minutes | Cook Time: 25 minutes | makes: 2 servings

Ingredients

- 2 gala apples, peeled and center cored
- 2 tablespoons of brown sugar
- 1/2 teaspoon cinnamon
- Pinch of salt
- Oil spray, for greasing

Directions

1. Wash and peel the apples.
2. Then center core the apples.
3. Take a mandolin apple cutter and cut the apples into thin slices.
4. In a bowl, mix apples, salt, brown sugar, and cinnamon.
5. Grease the mesh basket with oil spray.
6. Put the slices in the basket.
7. Set a timer to 40 minutes at 300 degrees F.
8. Air fry it until crisp, then takeout the apple.
9. Cool it for10 minutes, before serving.

Serving Suggestion: Serve it with ice-cream
Variation Tip: skip the sugar if want low Carb snack
Nutritional Information per Serving: Calories 105 | Fat 0.8 | Sodium 80mg | Carbs 25.3g | Fiber 2.3g | Sugar 22.7g | Protein 0.2g

Pineapple Crisp

Prep Time: 15 minutes | Cook Time: 25 minutes | makes: 2 servings

Ingredients

- 2 cups of pineapple rings
- 2 tablespoons of sugar, granulated
- ¼ teaspoon nutmeg
- Paprika, pinch
- Oil spray, for greasing

Directions

1. In a bowl, mix pineapples, salt, paprika, brown sugar, and nutmeg.
2. Grease the mesh basket with oil spray.
3. Put the pineapple slices in the basket.
4. Put the basket inside oven.
5. Set a timer to 60 minutes at 320 degrees F at air fry mode.
6. Once it crisp, takeout the pineapples and serve.

Serving Suggestion: Serve it with whipping cream
Variation Tip: skip the sugar if want low Carb snack
Nutritional Information per Serving: Calories 131 | Fat 0.6 | Sodium 2mg | Carbs 38g | Fiber 2.4g | Sugar 29g | Protein 0.9g

Eggless Cake

Prep Time: 15 minutes | Cook Time: 25 minutes | makes: 2 servings

Ingredients

- 1/3 cup all-purpose flour
- 4 tablespoons sugar, white
- 2 teaspoons vanilla extract
- Pinch of salt
- 2 tablespoons cocoa powder
- 1/8 teaspoon baking soda
- 4 tablespoons of coconut milk
- 2 tablespoons of olive oil
- 1 teaspoon warm water

Directions

1. First step is to Pre-heat the Ninja oven for 2 minutes at 300 degrees F.
2. Take a bowl and mix all the dry ingredients in it.
3. In a separate bowl, whisk egg and mix in all the wet liquid ingredients.
4. Now combine the ingredients of both the bowl.
5. Grease a cake pan with oil spray and pour the batter.
6. Place the cake pan in the preheated ninja oven and select the air fry mode for 12 minutes.
7. Insert a toothpick to check if the cake is done; else keep cooking for another few minutes.
8. Remove the cake pan and let it sit for 10 minutes before serving.
9. Enjoy.

Serving Suggestion: Serve it with ice-cream or drizzle of choclate syrup
Variation Tip: skip the sugar if want low Carb snack
Nutritional Information per Serving: Calories 397 | Fat 22.1 | Sodium 163mg | Carbs 46g | Fiber 3g | Sugar 26g | Protein 3g

Choclate Oatmeal Cookies

Prep Time: 15 minutes | Cook Time: 10 minutes | makes: 4 servings

Ingredients

- 2.5 Cups Quick-Cooking Oatmeal
- 1-1/2 Cups All-Purpose Flour
- 1/3 Cup Cocoa Powder
- 6 Ounces of Packet of Instant Chocolate Pudding Mix
- salt, to taste
- 1 Teaspoon Baking Soda
- 1 Cup Butter, Softened
- ½ Cup Brown Sugar
- 2 Eggs
- 1 Teaspoon Vanilla Extract
- 1 Cup Chocolate Chips
  Cooking Spray

Directions

1. Preheat the ninja oven to 350 degrees F for few minutes.
2. Spray the oven sheet with nonstick cooking spray.
3. Take a bowl and mix the flour, baking soda, oatmeal, cocoa powder, pudding mix, and salt.
4. Beat the butter, and brown sugar, in another bowl using hand beater.
5. Then add vanilla extract and eggs.
6. Add oatmeal and mix well.
7. Stir in chocolate chips and incorporate all the ingredients well.
8. Drop dough in the form of cookie scoop on baking sheet greased with oil spray
9. BAKE until lightly browned inside Ninja Foodi XL Pro Air Oven for 10 minutes.
10. Cool it on wire rack.
11. serve and enjoy.

Serving Suggestion: Serve it with coffee
Variation Tip: skip the sugar if want low Carb snack
Nutritional Information per Serving: Calories 1200 | Fat 64 | Sodium 1600mg | Carbs 142.9g | Fiber 11.3g | Sugar 40g | Protein 18g

Chapter 6: Beef, Pork, and Lamb Recipes

Sugar Glaze Ham

Prep Time: 15 Minutes | Cook Time: 25 Minutes | Makes: 4 Servings

Ingredients

- 2 pounds of ham,
- 1/2 cup orange juice
- 1/4 cup mustard
- 1/4 cup brown sugar
- 1 teaspoon of cloves

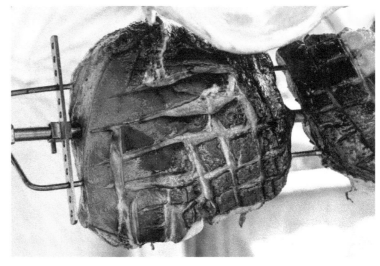

Directions

1. Preheat the Ninja Foodi XL Pro Air Oven to 350 degrees F, for a few minutes.
2. Take a bowl and combine cloves, mustard, brown sugar, orange juice.
3. Put the rotisserie shaft in the middle of the ham.
4. The next step is to tightly secure the forks.
5. Drizzle, the sauce over the ham.
6. Put it in the Ninja Foodi XL Pro Air Oven.
7. Now turn on the Ninja Foodi XL Pro Air Oven and press menu and select the air fry option and set the timer to 25 minutes at 400 degrees F.
8. Serve and enjoy.

Serving Suggestion: Serve it with favorite dipping sauce
Variation Tip: skip the sugar if want low Carb snack
Nutritional Information per Serving: Calories 466 | Fat 22.5 | Sodium 2600mg | Carbs 25 g | Fiber 5g | Sugar 12.1g | Protein 40.4g

Corned Beef and Cabbage Rolls

Prep Time: 15 minutes | Cook Time: 12 minutes | makes: 4 servings

Ingredients

- 8 egg rolls
- 1 pound corned beef, shredded
- 1 cup red cabbage. thinly sliced
- 6 tablespoons of Spicy mustard, as needed

Directions

1. Put the egg rolls on a flat surface.
2. Dump a heaping tablespoon of corned beef in middle and add cabbage and mustard about a tablespoon.
3. And place a small amount of corned beef in the center of the wrapper.
4. Add a small amount of cabbage, and mustard.
5. repeat the step for all wrappers.
6. Roll the wrappers.
7. Seal the edges with water.
8. Mist it with oil spray.
9. Layer the eggrolls on a rack of the Ninja Foodi XL Pro Air Oven.
10. Place it in the Ninja Foodi XL Pro Air Oven.
11. Press menu and select air fry.
12. Cook it for 12 minutes at 400 degrees F.
13. Remember to flip it halfway through.
14. Once it's done, serve.

Serving Suggestion: Serve it with salad or ketchup as dipping sauce.
Variation Tip: Non
Nutritional Information per Serving: Calories 400 | Fat 18.7 | Sodium 1334mg | Carbs 36g | Fiber 2.6g | Sugar 3g | Protein 21.8g

Lamb in Ninja Foodie Oven

Prep Time: 15 minutes | Cook Time: 22 minutes | makes: 5 servings

Ingredients

- ¼ tablespoon of lemon zest and juice
- Salt and black pepper, to taste
- 3 garlic cloves, minced
- ¼ cup mint, fresh
- ½ cup butter, melted
- 10 lamb chops

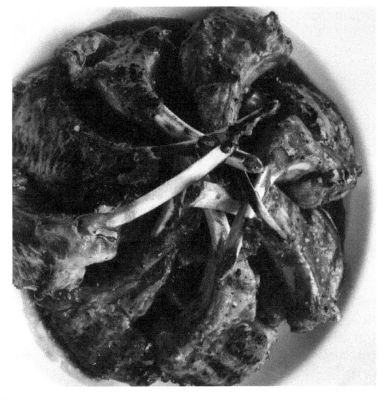

Directions

1. Take a bowl and lemon juice, salt, pepper lemon zest, garlic cloves, mint, and butter.
2. Rub this over the lamb and coat the lamb well.
3. Marinate the lamb for a few hours.
4. Put the lamb on the rack.
5. put rack inside oven.
6. Press menu and select bake.
7. Bake it for 22 at 390 degrees F.
8. Flip the lamb halfway through.
9. Once done, serve and enjoy.

Serving Suggestion: Serve it with coleslaw.
Variation Tip: None
Nutritional Information per Serving: Calories 688 | Fat 48 | Sodium 132mg | Carbs 11g | Fiber 0.4g | Sugar 0g | Protein 50.5 g

Salt and Black Pepper Steak

Prep Time: 15 minutes | Cook Time: 15 minutes | makes: 2 servings

Ingredients

- 2 sirloin steaks
- Salt and black pepper, to taste
- 4 tablespoons of melted butter

Directions

1. Rub the steak with butter, salt, and black pepper.
2. .
3. Grease the basket of Foodi XL Pro Air Oven with oil spray.
4. Put the steak in the basket.
5. Air fry for 15 minutes at 400 degrees F.
6. Once done, serve and enjoy.

Serving Suggestion: Serve it with roasted vegetables or mashed potatoes
Variation Tip: None
Nutritional Information per Serving: Calories 694 | Fat 57 | Sodium 284mg | Carbs 0.1g | Fiber 0g | Sugar 0g | Protein 43g

Pork Chops

Prep Time: 15 minutes | Cook Time: 18 minutes | makes: 2 servings

Ingredients

- 25 grams of brown sugar
- Salt and black pepper, to taste
- 4 tablespoons of bourbon
- 4 pork chops

Directions

1. In a medium saucepan, heat the brown sugar, bourbon, salt, and black pepper.
2. Heat it over a low flame.
3. Marinate the pork in it for a few minutes.
4. Now cover the baking tray with aluminum foil.
5. Put the pork on the baking tray.
6. put the tray inside Ninja Foodi XL Pro Air Oven.
7. Preheat the Ninja Foodi XL Pro Air Oven for 4 minutes at 400 degrees F.
8. Set the timer at 390 degrees F, for 18 minutes on air fry mode.
9. Once done, serve and enjoy.

Serving Suggestion: Serve it with mashed potatoes
Variation Tip: Skip the bourbon and add lime juice.
Nutritional Information per Serving: Calories 624 | Fat 40 | Sodium 116mg | Carbs 12g | Fiber 0g | Sugar 12.1g | Protein 36g

Rump Steak

Prep Time: 15 Minutes | Cook Time: 10 Minutes | Makes: 2 Servings

Ingredients

- 2 pounds of rump steak
- 2onions, sliced
- 1 green bell pepper, sliced
- Salt and black pepper, to taste
- ½ cup parmesan cheese
- 4 Hoagies roll, as needed

Directions

1. Take a Ninja Foodi XL Pro Air Oven and grease it with a mesh tray.
2. Place the steak, bell pepper, and onion in a bowl and season it with salt and black pepper.
3. Then place it on a baking tray.
4. Preheat the Ninja Foodi XL Pro Air Oven for 390 degrees F for 5 minutes.
5. Put the tray in the oven and Bake for 10 minutes at 350 degrees F.
6. Once done, place it on a hoagie roll and layer the shredded parmesan on top.
7. Serve and enjoy.

Serving Suggestion: Serve it with roasted vegetables
Variation Tip: skip cheese for low calories meal
Nutritional Information per Serving: Calories 1565 | Fat 52 | Sodium 1801mg | Carbs 102g | Fiber 17g | Sugar 15g | Protein 187.5g

Meat Patties

Prep Time: 15 minutes | Cook Time: 18 minutes | makes: 3 servings

Ingredients

- 1.5 pounds of grounded beef
- 2 tablespoons of olive oil
- 1/4 cup shallots
- 2 green peppers, chopped
- 1/3 teaspoon of cumin
- Oil spray, for greasing
- salt and black pepper, to taste

Directions

1. In a large bowl, combine grounded beef, salt, cumin, pepper, shallots, olive oil, and green pepper.
2. Make the meat patties with wet hands.
3. Mist the meat patties with oil spray.
4. Put it on to mesh tray of Ninja Foodi XL Pro Air Oven.
5. Bake at 375 degrees for 18 minutes.
6. Serve and enjoy.

Serving Suggestion: Serve it with ice-cream
Variation Tip: Add ginger garlic paste for extra flavor.
Nutritional Information per Serving: Calories 236 | Fat 17 | Sodium 52mg | Carbs 6g | Fiber 1.4g | Sugar 1.9g | Protein 14.1g

Teriyaki Glazed Steak

Prep Time: 15 minutes | Cook Time: 25 minutes | makes: 2 servings

Ingredients

- 4 beef Steaks

Teriyaki Glaze Ingredients

- 1/3 cup Soy Sauce
- ½ cup Japanese cooking wine
- 1/3 cup Brown Sugar
- 4 tablespoons Lime Juice
- 1/4 cup Orange Juice
- ½ teaspoon Ginger, ground
- ½ teaspoon of minced garlic

Directions

1. Combine the glaze ingredients in a bowl and transfer it to a sauce pan
2. Heat it over a low flame.
3. Let it cook for 5 minutes.
4. Coat the steak with glaze and let it marinate for 2 hours.
5. Put it on a baking tray and add it to the Ninja Foodi XL Pro Air Oven.
6. select bake and set the timer to 15 minutes at 392 degrees F.
7. Once done, serve and enjoy.

Serving Suggestion: Serve it with rice and mashed potato
Variation Tip: Skip the orange juice and add lemon zest.
Nutritional Information per Serving: Calories 508 | Fat 23 | Sodium 1344mg | Carbs 15.4g | Fiber 0.2g | Sugar 13.4g | Protein 55.1g

Country Style Ribs

Prep Time: 15 minutes | Cook Time: 18 minutes | makes: 2 servings

Ingredients

- 4 country-style pork ribs, trimmed excess fat

Marinate Ingredients

- 2 tablespoons cornstarch
- 2 tablespoons coconut oil
- 2 teaspoons dry mustard
- 1/4 teaspoon thyme
- ½ teaspoon garlic powder
- ½ teaspoon dried marjoram
- Salt and black pepper, to taste

Directions

1. In a bowl, mix all the marinade ingredients.
2. Marinate the pork ribs in it for a few hours.
3. Place the ribs onto the aluminum foiled baking tray.
4. Air Roast it for 18 minutes at 390 degrees F in Ninja Oven
5. Once done, serve and enjoy.

Serving Suggestion: Serve it with BBQ sauce
Variation Tip: use butter instead of oil
Nutritional Information per Serving: Calories 1119 | Fat 38 | Sodium 381mg | Carbs 9.2 g | Fiber 0.3g | Sugar 0.4g | Protein 175g

Steak and Mushroom Gravy

Prep Time: 15 minutes | Cook Time: 10 minutes | makes: 3 servings

Ingredients

- 1/3 cup olive oil
- 2 tablespoons coconut amino
- 3 teaspoons Montreal steak seasoning
- 1 teaspoon garlic powder
- 1.5 pounds of beef steaks cut into 3/4-inch pieces
- ¼ cup cream of mushroom soup

Directions

1. Take a bowl and combine olive oil, coconut amino, steak seasoning, steak pieces, and garlic powder.
2. Let it sit for 20 minutes.
3. Preheat the Ninja Foodi XL Pro Air Oven to 390 degrees F for 5 minutes.
4. Line the bottom of the Ninja Foodi XL Pro Air Oven baking tray with parchment paper.
5. Put the steak with marinade on to the tray.
6. Add cream of mushroom soup as well.
7. Stir all well.
8. Bake for 10 minutes.
9. Once done, serve and enjoy.

Serving Suggestion: Serve it over rice
Variation Tip: use soy sauce instead of coconut amino
Nutritional Information per Serving: Calories 632 | Fat 42 | Sodium 226mg | Carbs 1.4g | Fiber 0.1g | Sugar 0.4g | Protein 59g

Mongolian Beef

Prep Time: 15 minutes | Cook Time: 10 minutes | makes: 2 servings

Ingredients

- 1 pound of flank steak
- 1/4 cup corn starch

Sauce Ingredients

- 4 teaspoons of vegetable oil
- 1 teaspoon of ginger garlic paste
- 1/4 cup soy sauce or gluten-free soy sauce
- 1/4 cup water
- 1/2 cup brown sugar

Directions

1. Mix all the sauce ingredients in the bowl and coat the steak with it.
2. Let it marinate for 1 hour.
3. Preheat the ninja oven for 5minutes at 400 degrees F.
4. Now coat the steak with corn starch and put it on to the baking tray lined with aluminum foil.
5. Put it in the Ninja Foodi XL Pro Air Oven and bake for 10 minutes at 400 degrees F.

Serving Suggestion: Serve it with rice.
Variation Tip: skip the soy sauce and add coconut amino.
Nutritional Information per Serving: Calories 745 | Fat 28 | Sodium 2000mg | Carbs 56g | Fiber 0.3g | Sugar 35g | Protein 65g

Lamb Chops in Yogurt

Prep Time: 90 minutes | Cook Time: 15 minutes | makes: 2 servings

Ingredients

- 1 cup low-fat yogurt, side serving
- ½ teaspoon of cumin powder
- ½ tablespoon of coriander powder
- 1/3 teaspoon chili powder
- ½ teaspoon GaramMasala powder
- 1 tablespoon lemon juice
- ¼ teaspoon salt
- Black pepper, to taste
- 4 lamb chops, bone-in

Directions

1. Take a bowl and mix yogurt, lemon juice, cumin, salt, pepper, coriander powder, chili powder.
2. And garam Masala powder.
3. Marinate the lamb chops in it for 60 minutes.
4. Put the lamb chops in a baking pan that is lined with aluminum foil, and bake it for 15 minutes in Ninja Foodi XL Pro Air Oven.
5. Once done, serve and enjoy.

Serving Suggestion: Serve it with ranch
Variation Tip: None.
Nutritional Information per Serving: Calories 1309 | Fat 50 | Sodium 880mg | Carbs 10g | Fiber 0.3g | Sugar 10g | Protein 190g

Chapter 7: Vegetables and Sides Recipes

Buffalo Cauliflower

Prep Time: 15 minutes | Cook Time: 22 minutes | makes: 2 servings

Ingredients

- 1 head of cauliflower
- Salt and black pepper, to taste
- 1 tablespoon of olive oil
- 1 tablespoon of lemon juice
- 1 cup buffalo sauce

Directions

1. Preheat the ninja oven to 350 degrees F for a few minutes.
2. Then wash and pat dry the cauliflower florets.
3. Take a bowl and mix all the ingredients with the cauliflower.
4. Coat the cauliflowers and then layer them on a baking sheet.
5. Place baking sheet on Ninja Foodi XL Pro Air Oven and select bake for 360 degrees F, at 22 minutes.
6. Once done, serve.

Serving Suggestion: Serve it ketchup
Variation Tip: Skip the lemon juice and use vinegar.
Nutritional Information per Serving: Calories 95 | Fat 7.2 | Sodium 41mg | Carbs 8g | Fiber 3.4g | Sugar 3.3g | Protein 3g

Stuffed Shells

Prep Time: 15 minutes | Cook Time: 25 minutes | makes: 2 servings

Ingredients

- 1 package dry pasta jumbo shells
- 2.5 pounds ricotta cheese
- 1 cup kale
- 1/2 bag spinach
- 1 jar marinara sauce
- ½ cup grated Parmesan cheese
- oil spray, for greasing

Directions

1. Take a baking sheet and grease it oil spray.
2. Fill the shells with cheese, and arrange it on a sheet pan facing the cheese-side up.
3. Take a bowl and marinara sauce, kale, and spinach.
4. Fill it into shells.
5. Select BAKE functions of Ninja Foodi XL Pro Air Oven, and adjust the time to 390 degrees F for 25 minutes.
6. Place sheet pan in ninja oven.
7. Press START/PAUSE to begin.
8. Once done, serve and enjoy.

Serving Suggestion: Serve it with roasted vegetables.
Variation Tip: Use any other cheese variation.
Nutritional Information per Serving: Calories 1400 | Fat 50 | Sodium 788mg | Carbs 167g | Fiber 3g | Sugar 7g | Protein 88g

Roasted Green Beans

Prep Time: 20 minutes | Cook Time: 20 minutes | makes: 2 servings

Ingredients

- 4 slices prosciutto
- ¼ pound green beans, ends trimmed
- 1 small yellow onion, sliced
- 1 tablespoon canola oil

Directions

1. Preheat the Ninja Foodi XL Pro Air Oven to 350 degrees F for few minutes.
2. In a ninja oven basket and put prosciutto and bake it for 5 minutes at 390 degrees.
3. Take a bowl and mix the remaining ingredients.
4. take out the prosciutto from the oven.
5. Put the vegetables in an oven basket and air fry it for15 more minutes
6. crumble the prosciutto and sprinkle it on top of roasted green beans
7. Enjoy.

Serving Suggestion: Serve it with mashed potatoes
Variation Tip: Use olive oil instead of canola oil.
Nutritional Information per Serving: Calories 213 | Fat 13 | Sodium 1405mg | Carbs 8g | Fiber 2.7g | Sugar 2.3g | Protein 17g

Spinach and Broccoli

Prep Time: 15 minutes | Cook Time: 20 minutes | makes: 4 servings

Ingredients

- 1.5 cups of spinach leaves, stem removed
- ½ cup broccoli florets
- 4 tablespoons of canola oil
- Salt, to taste
- Black pepper, to taste
- 2 teaspoons of onion powder

Directions

1. Rinse and pat dry the spinach.
2. Remove the leaves of the spinach.
3. In a large bowl, toss spinach leaves with canola oil, broccoli, black, salt, and onion powder.
4. Toss the ingredients and put the ingredients in a mesh basket.
5. put the mesh basket in oven.
6. Select air fry and adjust the timer of ninja Oven for 20 minutes at 380 degrees F.
7. Once the timer is done, serve, and enjoy.

Serving Suggestion: Serve it with a sprinkle of parmesan shavings
Variation Tip: Add vegetables of your own choice more.
Nutritional Information per Serving: Calories 134 | Fat 15 | Sodium 52mg | Carbs 1.2g | Fiber 0.6g | Sugar 0.2g | Protein 0.6g

Blooming Onion

Prep Time: 15 minutes | Cook Time: 25 minutes | makes: 2 servings

Ingredients

- 1 large white onion
- Salt and black pepper, to taste
- 4 eggs, whisked
- 4 tablespoons of olive oil
- 1.5 cup Panko bread crumbs
- 1/4 teaspoon of garlic powder
- 1/4 teaspoon of paprika
- 1.5 cup flour

Directions

1. Peel the onions and cut the top.
2. Make slices of onion to the bottom.
3. Do not cut through the bottom, it should bloom open.
4. Dump it in the ice water for 2 hours.
5. In a bowl whisk egg.
6. In a bowl, and mix salt, paprika, garlic powder, black pepper, and flour.
7. Pat dry onion and then dredge the onion in flour, then in egg mix.
8. Again, coat it with flour mixture.
9. At the end coat it with bread crumbs.
10. Put it in a mesh basket and brush the onions with olive oil.
11. Bake it for 25 minutes at 390 degrees Fahrenheit.
12. Serve and enjoy.

Serving Suggestion: Serve it with   ranch
Variation Tip: None
Nutritional Information per Serving: Calories 1059 | Fat 42 | Sodium 721mg | Carbs 138g | Fiber 7.6g | Sugar 10g | Protein 32g

Sweet Potato Fries

Prep Time: 15 minutes | Cook Time: 30 minutes | makes: 4 servings

Ingredients

- 4 sweet potatoes, cut it into wedges
- 2 tablespoons of olive oil
- salt, to taste

Directions

1. Soak the potato slices in cold water for 30 minutes.
2. pat dry potatoes slices and let them get dry
3. Season it with salt and oil.
4. Layer it in a baking sheet and bake in Ninja Foodi XL Pro Air Oven for 30 minutes at 390 degrees F.
5. Serve and enjoy.

Serving Suggestion: Serve it with ketchup or cheese sauce.
Variation Tip: Use butter instead of olive oil.
Nutritional Information per Serving: Calories 172 | Fat 7.3 | Sodium 110mg | Carbs 26g | Fiber 3.9g | Sugar 54g | Protein 2.3g

Potato Tots

Prep Time: 15 minutes | Cook Time: 22 minutes | makes: 4 servings

Ingredients

- 8 potato tots
- 8 bacon strips
- 4 scallions
- Oil spray, for greasing

Directions

1. Preheat the Ninja Foodi XL Pro Air Oven to 350 degrees F for few minutes.
2. Grease a baking pan with oil spray.
3. Wrap each potato tots with one bacon strip; put it on a baking pan.
4. Put the baking pan in the Ninja Foodi XL Pro Air Oven.
5. Chose the air fry and press the start.
6. Set a timer to 22 minutes at 390 degrees F.
7. Once the cooking cycle complete, take out the potato tart and serve with chopped scallions.

Serving Suggestion: Serve it sour cream
Variation Tip: skip the scallions as a garnishing ingredient.
Nutritional Information per Serving: Calorie 805 | Fat 37 | Sodium 1460mg | Carbs 108g | Fiber 10g | Sugar 48g | Protein 10g

Corn on a Cob

Prep Time: 25 minutes | Cook Time: 20 minutes | makes: 2 servings

Ingredients

- 2 corn on a cob
- 2 tablespoons for butter
- Salt and black pepper

Directions

1. Preheat the Ninja Foodi XL Pro Air Oven to 350 degrees F, for few minutes.
2. Rub the corn cobs with salt, pepper, and butter.
3. Put in on baking sheet layer with aluminum foil.
4. Bake it inside Ninja Foodi XL Pro Air Oven for 20 minutes at 400 degrees F.
5. Once done, serve.

Serving Suggestion: Serve it with lemon squeeze
Variation Tip: use olive oil instead of butter.
Nutritional Information per Serving: Calories 191 | Fat 7.5 | Sodium 58mg | Carbs 31.9g | Fiber 1g | Sugar 0g | Protein 4.6g

Baked Eggplants

Prep Time: 15 Minutes | Cook Time: 4 Hours | Makes: 2 Servings

Ingredients

- 2 large eggplants
- 2 tablespoons of olive oil

Spice Ingredients

- 1 teaspoon of cumin
- ¼ teaspoon of turmeric
- ¼ teaspoon of Garam Masala
- salt and black pepper, to taste

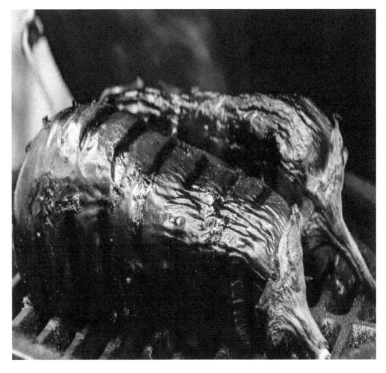

Directions

1. Preheat the Ninja Foodi XL Pro Air Oven to 350 degrees F for few minutes.
2. Mix all the spices in a bowl.
3. Cut open the eggplants by making 4 slits, till the end.
4. Remember not to reach the bottom.
5. Brush it with olive oil and rub the prepared seasonings all over the eggplants.
6. Put it on a baking sheet that is covered with aluminum foil
7. Air fry in Ninja Foodi XL Pro Air Oven for 4 hours at 210 degrees F.
8. Serve and enjoy.

Serving Suggestion: Serve it with a sprinkle of parmesan shaving
Variation Tip: use canola oil instead of olive oil
Nutritional Information per Serving: Calories 262 | Fat 15.5 | Sodium 13mg | Carbs32 g | Fiber 16.5g | Sugar 16g | Protein 5.6g

Zucchini Crisps

Prep Time: 15 minutes | Cook Time: 18 minutes | makes: 2 servings

Ingredients

- 16 tablespoons of water
- Sea Salt, to taste
- ¼ teaspoon of Paprika, pinch
- Red chili flakes, to taste
- 2 zucchinis, peeled, round sliced
- ½ cup chickpea flour
- Oil spray, for greasing

Directions

1. Take a large bowl and mix water, sea salt paprika, red chili flakes, and chickpea flour in it.
2. Put the sliced zucchini into the chickpea flour.
3. Coat it well and layer it in a basket.
4. Air fry it in Ninja Foodi XL Pro Air Oven for about 15-18 minutes at 390 degrees F.
5. During cooking, shake the basket twice.
6. Remember chips do not overlap.
7. Serve it once done.

Serving Suggestion: Serve it with   ketchup
Variation Tip: Skip the chilies, if not like spicy food.
Nutritional Information per Serving: Calories 217 | Fat 3.7 | Sodium 150mg | Carbs 37g | Fiber 11g | Sugar 8g | Protein 12g

Cheddar Biscuits

Prep Time: 15 Minutes | Cook Time: 22 Minutes | Makes: 2 Servings

Ingredients

- ½ cup flour
- ½ stick of butter, melted
- ½ cup of scallion
- 1 cup cheddar cheese
- ½ cup buttermilk
- 1 teaspoon of baking soda
- ½ teaspoon of seafood seasoning

Directions

1. Take a bowl and combine melted butter with flour.
2. Mix it well to form a crumble.
3. Then pour in the buttermilk, baking soda, seas food seasoning, cheddar cheese, scallion and mix well.
4. Divide the mixture into equal round shapes and layer it on a baking sheet greased with oil spray
5. put it in Ninja Foodi XL Pro Air Oven and select bake function.
6. Set time to 22 minutes at 360 degrees F.
7. Once done, serve and enjoy.

Serving Suggestion: Serve it with butter
Variation Tip: Skip the scallions
Nutritional Information per Serving: Calories 577 | Fat 42.5 | Sodium 1212mg | Carbs 29g | Fiber 1.8g | Sugar 3g | Protein 20g

Chapter 8: Meal Plan

Days	Breakfast	Lunch	Dinner
Day1	Cereal French toast	Pork Chops Corn On A Cob	Chicken Tikka Masala
Day 2	French toast Sticks	Mongolian Beef Baked Eggplants	Baked Eggplants
Day 3	Breakfast Hash	Lamb Chops In Yogurt	Pork Chops
Day 4	Air Fryer Perfect Cinnamon Toast	Chicken Stir Fry	Rump Steak
Day 5	Breakfast Soufflé	Chicken Meat Patties	Meat Patties Chocolate Peanut Butter Cupcakes
Day 6	Breakfast Frittata Recipe	Teriyaki Glazed Chicken	Teriyaki Glazed Steak Corn On A Cob
Day 7	Avocado Eggs	Whole Chicken Roast Blooming Onion	Country Style Ribs Cheddar Biscuits
Day 8	Breakfast Oats	BBQ Chicken Wings & Pineapple Crisp	Stuffed Shells &Roasted Green Beans

Day 9	DELICIOUS EGG AND CHEESE MUFFINS	CHICKEN STIR FRY	COUNTRY STYLE CHICKEN WINGS
Day 10	Delicious Egg And Cheese Muffins	FISH FILLET IN AIR FRYER	ROASTED CHICKEN WITH APPLE
Day 11	BANANA CUPCAKE	GINGER GARLIC SALMON	TARRAGON-MUSTARD CHICKEN
Day 12	CHOCOLATE PEANUT BUTTER CUPCAKES	TEMPURA BATTER FISH	CHEESY CHICKEN
Day 13	CHOCLATE OATMEAL COOKIES	ZESTY LEMON SALMON	CAJUN SPICE CHICKEN
Day 14	BREAKFAST SOUFFLÉ	FISH FILLET IN AIR FRYER	COUNTRY STYLE CHICKEN WINGS
Day 15	BREAKFAST FRITTATA RECIPE	COUNTRY STYLE RIBS	LEMON & HERB PANKO CRUSTED COD
Day 16	AVOCADO EGGS	STEAK AND MUSHROOM GRAVY	COCONUT FISH FILLET
Day 17	BREAKFAST OATS	MONGOLIAN BEEF	COCONUT MILK SHRIMP
Day 18	DELICIOUS EGG AND CHEESE MUFFINS	LAMB CHOPS IN YOGURT	LEMON & HERB PANKO CRUSTED COD
Day 19	Delicious Egg And Cheese Muffins	TERIYAKI GLAZED CHICKEN	COCONUT FISH FILLET
Day 20	BREAKFAST SOUFFLÉ	WHOLE CHICKEN ROAST	COCONUT MILK SHRIMP
Day 21	BREAKFAST FRITTATA RECIPE	BBQ CHICKEN WINGS	TERIYAKI GLAZED CHICKEN

Conclusion

No doubt the Ninja Foodi XL Pro Air Oven is an all in one appliance that makes cooking healthier, easy, and fun.

Now you can stop spending your extra dollar to buy multiple appliances to do several cooking jobs, as the Ninja Foodi XL Pro Air Oven can do magic for you.

We hope this guide makes you prepare and use the function and temperate of the appliance for specific recipes and create an ease of accessibly in day-to-day cooking.

CPSIA information can be obtained
at www.ICGtesting.com
Printed in the USA
LVHW060514270121
677608LV00003B/114

.